Noah
and the incredible flood

Janis Hansen
illustrated by wendy francisco

CROSSWAY BOOKS • WHEATON, ILLINOIS
A DIVISION OF GOOD NEWS PUBLISHERS

ROBIN ROAD PRODUCTIONS
SHERMAN OAKS, CALIFORNIA

Dedicated
to all the little children of the world

OTHER BIBLE ADVENTURE CLUB STORIES

Creation: God's Wonderful Gift

David and His Giant Battle

Jonah and His Amazing Voyage

Jesus: The Birthday of the King

Noah and the Incredible Flood
Text and illustrations copyright © 2001 by Robin Road Productions
Published by Crossway Books, a division of Good News Publishers,
1300 Crescent Street, Wheaton, Illinois 60187

Illustrations: Wendy Francisco
First printing 2001
Printed in the United States of America

Library of Congress Cataloging-in-Publication Data
Hansen, Janis (Janis S.), 1942-
  Noah and the incredible flood / Janis Hansen ; illustrated by
Wendy Francisco.
      p   cm. - (Bible Adventure club)
  Summary: Noah obeys God's commandments and saves
himself, his family, and two of each kind of animal in the world
from a devastating flood.
  ISBN 1-58134-339-6 (alk. paper)
  1. Noah's ark-Juvenile literature. [1. Noah (Biblical figure).
  2. Noah's ark. 3. Bible stories-O.T.] I. Francisco, Wendy, ill.
  II. Title.
BS658 .H29 2001
222'.1109505-dc21   2001002271
                                                                  CIP

15 14 13 12 11 10 09 08 07 06 05 04 03 02 01
15 14 13 12 11 10 9 8 7 6 5 4 3 2 1

Welcome to Noah's Bible Adventure!

We're sure the kids in your life will love the journey they're about to embark on. From the great storybook and audio-cassette to the fun-filled activity book and interactive CD-Rom, your young adventurers will discover the story of *Noah* in a new and exciting way. And the "Parents' Guide" will help you play a vital role in their experience.

Because what and how kids learn is important to us, we've had every element of *Noah and the Incredible Flood* reviewed by both a religious and an educational board of advisors. The content and vocabulary are appropriate for young children, and will help them develop reading and language skills, which are the cornerstones of education. Kids will also be able to expand and nourish their creativity as each Bible Adventure Club product challenges them to use their imagination. And most importantly, the knowledge they learn in these stories of God's Word will enhance their growing faith.

So begin with the great adventure stories of the Bible and start kids on a path that will enrich their lives in both faith and knowledge. And with you by their side, it'll be a fun-filled journey that you all will remember!

In the very beginning, God created our beautiful world.
He made mountains and trees and animals and good people.

Over the years, the people forgot
about God and became unkind.
God was very sad.

God searched the whole world, but the only good people He could find were Noah and his family!

"Noah, I've decided to cover the whole world with water and make a new start.

So build a huge boat called an ark; then round up all the animals, two by two, and load them on the ark. Then you and your family get on board. Do you understand?"

"Yes, God. I see. The ark will be a sort of floating zoo!"

Noah and his sons began building the huge ark just the way God wanted them to.

Soon everyone heard about Noah and his ark.

"Look at that strange Noah!"

"He's building a boat, and there's no place to sail it!"

"I'm building an ark so we can be saved. God told me He's sending a terrible flood."

"Did you hear that? Now he's hearing voices!"

They couldn't imagine such a huge flood!

"Finally the ark is finished!"
"And just in time, Noah. Here come the children with the animals!"

"Bringing in the animals
Two by two,
Bears and bats and bandicoots, to name a few,
Wallabies and llamas, pandas and iguanas—
Every kind of creature in the world."

"Loading up the animals
Two by two; why, there's
Elephants and marmosets and kangaroos,
Tigers and gorillas, zebras and chinchillas,
Crocodiles and bumblebees—
Let them get on board please.
We've got a job to do!
Loading up the animals
Two by two!"

Noah's family helped all the animals get ready for their long journey.

The animals were at peace with one
another because they were part of
God's plan.

As dark clouds appeared, God spoke to Noah again. "Now is the time, Noah. Take Mrs. Noah and join your family on board."

God started the rain.

Lightning split the heavens, and thunder shook
the earth.

The rain began to form pools of water. The pools
of water became streams, and the streams turned
into rivers!

Rivers rose and everything flooded with water, and
soon Noah's ark floated alone upon the growing sea.

It rained and rained for forty days and forty nights.

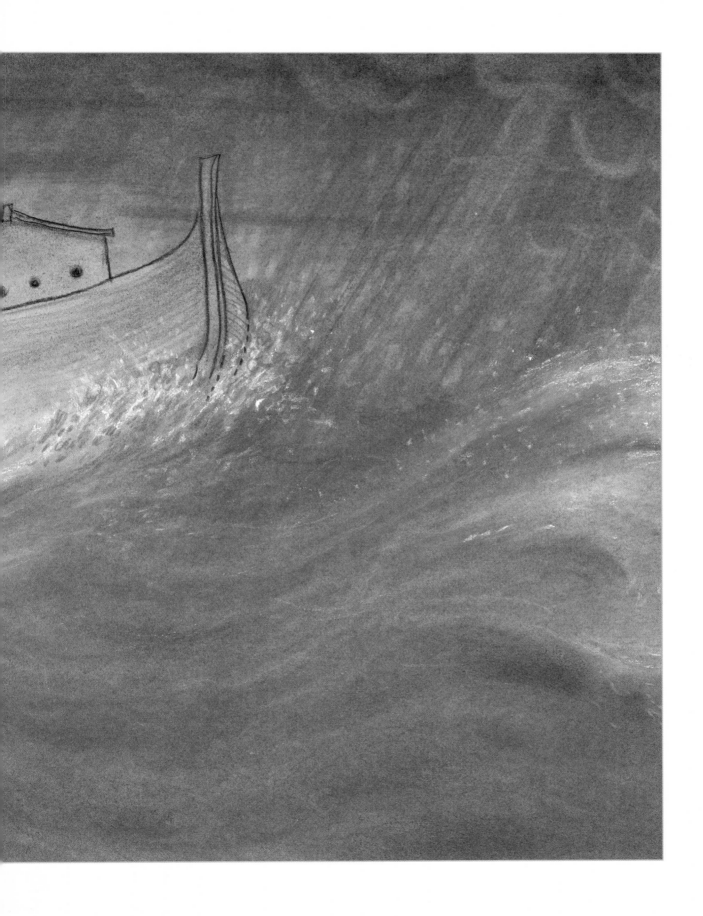

Aboard the ark everyone was safe and dry.

Early one morning, Noah
awakened with a start.
"Wife, listen! Something's different!"
"I don't hear anything, Noah."
"Well, that's just it! Wake up everyone!
Praise God! The rain has stopped!"

As the ark floated on the water with no land in sight, God sent a gentle wind to dry the earth.

Slowly the tips of mountains began to appear. After 150 days, Noah's ark came to rest upon a mountain called Ararat.

After forty more days, Noah sent a dove out into the cool air.

"Little Dove, look for dry land. If anyone can find it, you can!"

The dove could find no dry land. She flew back to the ark at the end of the day.

Seven days later Noah sent Little Dove to look for land again.

"Look, everyone, it's our Little Dove,
and she has an olive twig in her beak!
That means trees are above the water!"

Noah waited seven more days and sent out the dove again.

"Well, we've waited for Little Dove all day, and she still hasn't come back, and the land looks dry to me!"

Once more God spoke to Noah.

"You have done your job well, Noah. You may now leave the ark. Release all the creatures so they may find their new homes."

"The world is alive again!"

"Thank You for saving us, God.
We promise to obey You and be good
to each other.

And we'll take care of this beautiful earth and all
Your creatures."

God was pleased and spread a beautiful rainbow
across the sky.

"From now on, when you see a rainbow, it will
remind you of My promise that I will never again
send such a terrible flood."

God blessed Noah and his family, and they lived
happily.